MARVELS OF TECHNOLOGY

BODY & HEALTH TECH

by
Anita Loughrey and Alex Woolf

Minneapolis, Minnesota

Credits

Cover and title page, © Real Sports Photos/Shutterstock and , © kanpisut/Shutterstock and © KrulUA/iStock; 4MR, © Rawpixel.com/Shutterstock; 4BR, © StockPhotoPro/Adobe Stock; 4–5, © Gorodenkoff/Shutterstock; 6, © Designua/Shutterstock; 6–7, © Andrey_Popov/Shutterstock; 7TL, © W.J. Stacey/Wellcome collection; 7MR, © Henrik Dolle/Shutterstock; 7BR, © Titikul_B/Shutterstock; 8, © MONOPOLY919/Shutterstock; 8–9, © Pongsakorn/Adobe Stock 8–9, © Kjetil Kolbjornsrud/Shutterstock; 9ML, © Ground Picture/Shutterstock; 9BL, © Glogger/Wikimedia Commons; 10M, © Martin Sanders/Beehive Illustration; 10BL, © George Grantham Bain Collection, US Library of Congress/Wikimedia Commons; 10-11, © Africa Studio/Shutterstock; 11TR, © Barry Barnes/Shutterstock; 11BR, © VisitBritain/Pawel Libera/Getty Images; 12TR, © anaken2012/Shutterstock; 12ML, © Steve Heap/Shutterstock; 12MB, © dmytro herasymeniuk/Shutterstock; 12–13, © DenPhotos/Shutterstock; 13BL, © Dr. Dietrich Matthes/; 14MR, © DenPhotos/Shutterstock; 14–15, © oneinchpunch/Adobe Stock; 15BR, © Kyodo/Associated Press; 16MR, © Tewan Banditrakkanka/Shutterstock; 16BL, © Click and Photo/Shutterstock; 16–17, © Black Duck Style/Shutterstock; 17BL, © Wellcome collection; 18TR, © pics five/Shutterstock; 18ML, © BlueRingMedia/Shutterstock; 18BR, © Martin Sanders/Beehive Illustration; 18–19, © bluebay/Shutterstock; 19TL, © AlexLMX/Shutterstock; 19MR, © Martin Sanders/Beehive Illustration; 19, © Alexonline/Shutterstock; 20MR, © Mopic/Shutterstock; 20BL, © Rvector/Shutterstock; 20–21, © Real Sports Photos/Shutterstock; 21BR, © SolStock/istock; 22TR, © Smile111222/Wikimedia Commons; 22L, © Sean Dempsey - PA Images/Getty Images; 22–23, © BERTRAND GUAY/Getty Images; 23TL, © FPG / Staff/Getty Images; 24TR, © Audio und werbung/Shutterstock; 24MR, © NosorogUA/Shutterstock; 24–25, © Corepics VOF/Shutterstock; 25TL, © Timothy Fadek/Getty Images; 26M, © sfam_photo/Shutterstock; 26BL, © Grzegorz Placzek/Shutterstock; 26–27, © Juice Verve/Shutterstock; 27BL, © Wellcome collection; 28BL, © BlueRingMedia/Shutterstock; 28–29, © KaliAntye/Shutterstock; 29TL, © Net Vector/Shutterstock; 29MR, © Dmitry Kalinovsky/Shutterstock; 29BL, © MriMan/Shutterstock; 30ML, © ktsdesign/Shutterstock; 30BL, © Jemastock/Shutterstock; 30–31, © adike/Shutterstock; 31TL, © nobeastsofierce/Shutterstock; 31BL, © Ivonne Wierink/Shutterstock; 32M, © BigBlueStudio/Shutterstock; 32BL, © Alona Siniehina/Shutterstock; 32BR, © fotografos/Shutterstock; 32–33, © Stepan Popov/Dreamstime; 33TL, © Jeri Ellsworth/Wikimedia commons; 34M, © vetkit/Shutterstock; 34BL, © bsd studio/Shutterstock; 34–35, © Lucky Business/Shutterstock; 35BR, © Likee68/Shutterstock; 36BL, © Hallbauer & Fioretti; 36MR, © ibreakstock/Shutterstock; 36–37, © Marcin Balcerzak/Shutterstock; 37TL, © Africa Studio/Shutterstock; 37BL, © Hallbauer & Fioretti/; 38TR, © Johnny Dao/Shutterstock; 38MR, © Gorodenkoff/Shutterstock; 38BL, © VoodooDot/Shutterstock; 38-39, © Jenson/Shutterstock; 40BL, © LightField Studios/Shutterstock; 40–41, © Anton Gvozdikov/Shutterstock; 41TR, © Pack-Shot/Shutterstock; 41BL, © Www3cubed/Wikimedia commons; 42BL, © Andrey_Popov/Shutterstock; 42–43, © Gorodenkoff/Shutterstock; 43BR, © metamorworks/Shutterstock; 44BR, © StockPhotoPro/Adobe Stock; 45TR, © MriMan/Shutterstock; 45BR, © Tewan Banditrakkanka/Shutterstock; 47, © Johnny Dao/Shutterstock

Bearport Publishing Company Product Development Team

President: Jen Jenson; Director of Product Development: Spencer Brinker; Managing Editor: Allison Juda; Associate Editor: Naomi Reich; Associate Editor: Tiana Tran; Art Director: Colin O'Dea; Designer: Kim Jones; Designer: Kayla Eggert; Product Development Assistant: Owen Hamlin

Statement on Usage of Generative Artificial Intelligence

Bearport Publishing remains committed to publishing high-quality nonfiction books. Therefore, we restrict the use of generative AI to ensure accuracy of all text and visual components pertaining to a book's subject. See BearportPublishing.com for details.

Library of Congress Cataloging-in-Publication Data is available at www.loc.gov or upon request from the publisher.

ISBN: 979-8-89232-083-2 (hardcover)
ISBN: 979-8-89232-615-5 (paperback)
ISBN: 979-8-89232-216-4 (ebook)

For more information, write to Bearport Publishing, 5357 Penn Avenue South, Minneapolis, MN 55419.

Contents

What Tech Can Do

At its most basic, technology is simple. It's the application of scientific knowledge to create things that solve problems and make our lives easier, safer, and healthier. But what technology can do is pretty amazing.

Meeting Our Needs

New technologies are developed to meet needs that we have. For example, hearing loss and increasingly poor eyesight are common with aging. People used to just accept and live with these things. Then, inventors developed and continuously improved upon hearing aids and eyeglasses.

Solving Problems

Technology changes as our needs change. In many parts of the world, the population is aging quickly and there are not enough young people to care for these older adults. Engineers are busy designing and developing health-care robots that can diagnose illness, offer day-to-day care, and even provide companionship and conversation to the sick and elderly.

The advancement of computers allows technology to assist specific body parts after accidents or illnesses.

Designing the Human Body of Tomorrow

Every day, designers are working to solve human health problems by developing new and improved artificial body parts, repairing faulty genes, advancing imaging and diagnostic machinery, and implanting computer-connected smart devices in human bodies. The main goal is to improve the quality of human life while extending it for as long as possible.

Glasses

For someone with good eyesight, light travels into the eye and hits the lens of the eye. The lens focuses the light directly onto the retina at the back of the eyeball. If a person is farsighted, close-up objects look blurred because the lens of their eye focuses light behind the retina. A farsighted person needs glasses with convex lenses, which shorten the path of the light. If someone is shortsighted, distant objects appear blurred because the lens of their eye focuses light in front of the retina. These people need glasses with concave lenses, which lengthen the path of the light.

An optometrist checks the patient's eye and prescribes the lenses needed to see clearly.

Bifocals and Varifocals

Some people need glasses for seeing both long distances and close-up objects. Bifocal lenses in glasses have two parts to meet these different needs. Varifocal lenses gradually change from long-distance at the top to short-distance at the bottom.

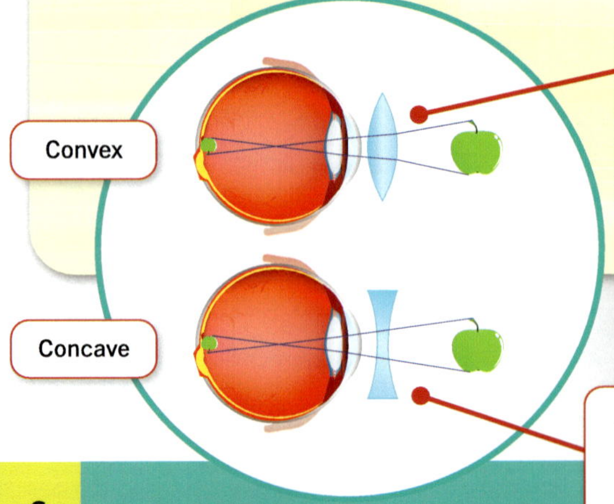

A convex lens in glasses causes the light to focus at a point closer to the eye's lens.

A concave lens in glasses causes the light rays to travel farther and focus farther from the lens.

INVENTOR

Inventor: Hermann von Helmholtz

Invention: Ophthalmoscope

Date: 1851

The story: German physicist Hermann von Helmholtz invented the ophthalmoscope. He wanted to discover why the pupil sometimes looks black and other times appears red.

Lens for examining patient's eye

Light to shine into patient's pupil

Focusing wheel

An ophthalmoscope lets an eye doctor inspect the back of the patient's eye to diagnose any problems.

Bridge

Arm

Lens

Nose cushion

Frame

DID YOU KNOW? Most eyeglass lenses are made from plastic that can be treated with a filter to protect eyes from ultraviolet rays from the sun.

Smartglasses

There was a time when a simple pair of eyeglasses was a marvel of technology, offering clear eyesight to those with blurry vision. But today, some glasses can do so much more than just help you see. Smartglasses are computers that you can wear. They can collect data from other devices using wireless technology while looking like an ordinary pair of eyeglasses!

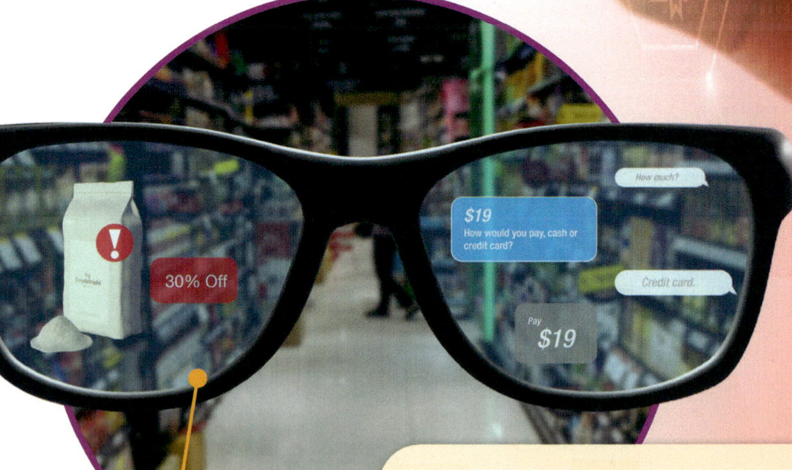

Smartglasses can provide the wearer with visual information about the world around them.

Smartglasses have many of the same features as a smartphone. Wearers can search the internet, get driving or walking directions, track their physical activity, take photographs, record videos, and play music. They can even send and receive texts, emails, and phone calls.

DID YOU KNOW? Some smart sunglasses can change their lens filters to adjust to changing light conditions, such as when a wearer moves from outdoors to indoors.

Smartglasses display images that appear to the wearer to float in space.

To be convenient and practical, smartglasses have to be as hands-free as possible. Different smartglasses can be operated by voice command, eye motions, gestures, or by using a smartphone as a remote control device. Developers are also working on ways to control smartglasses with brain activity so a user would only have to think of a command.

INVENTION

Inventor: Steve Mann

Invention: The Digital Eye Glass

Date: 1978

The story: Steve Mann is a Canadian engineer and inventor known as the father of wearable computing. By developing eyeglasses that incorporated a camera and TV display, he became a pioneer of wearable devices that perform multiple functions.

Hearing Aids

Hearing aids help bring out sounds from the world around people who have hearing loss. The two main kinds of hearing aid are analog and digital. Analog hearing aids convert sound waves into electrical signals, which are then amplified. Digital hearing aids convert sound waves into numerical codes before amplifying them.

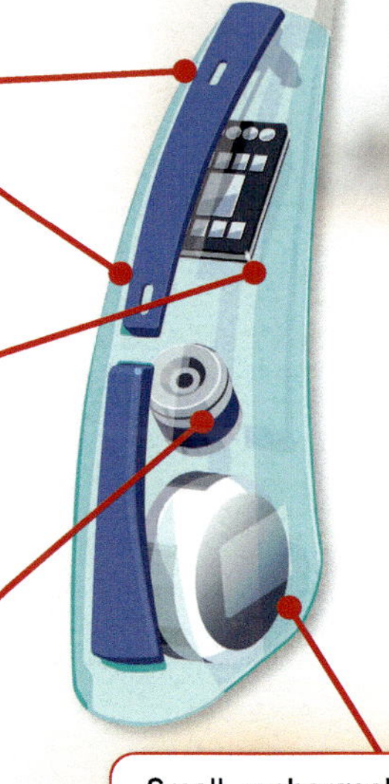

Telecoil

A telecoil is a small, magnetic coil inside a hearing aid. It helps the user hear conversations on a telephone. The telecoil also enables the user to connect to specialized sound systems that enhances sound quality in hearing aids.

INVENTOR

Inventor: Miller Reese Hutchison

Invention: First electronic hearing aid

Date: 1898

The story: Miller Reese Hutchison designed the first portable hearing aid, called Akouphone. In 1902, he made the more portable Acousticon. They both used a microphone from a telephone to amplify sound.

Induction Loop

An induction loop is a sound system found in public places, such as schools, theaters, concert halls, and airports. A loop of wire placed around a room produces an electromagnetic signal that can be received by hearing aids used by people who are partially deaf. When a person speaks into a microphone, the sound is amplified and sent to an antenna that relays the signal directly to the hearing aid. This eliminates background noise.

DID YOU KNOW? Hearing is dependent on tiny hairs and bones deep inside the ear.

Watches

Inside a quartz watch, a battery sends electricity to a quartz crystal, causing it to vibrate at a specific frequency. An electronic circuit converts the vibrations into electric pulses, one per second. These can cause a digital display to change or drive a small motor to turn the watch's hands. In addition to telling time, internet-connected smartwatches also let wearers receive notifications and track health data.

Digital Watches

Digital watches show the time using a liquid-crystal display. A computer in the watch tells it to reset back to 1:00:00 once it reaches 12:59:59.

Mechanical Watch

The inside of a mechanical watch is known as the movement. It has wheels and gears to turn hour, minute, and second hands on the watch face. Small jewels are used to reduce friction and help the gears move smoothly. These watches don't need electricity. Instead, they are powered by the user physically winding a spring, known as a mainspring.

DID YOU KNOW? The Rolex Deepsea Challenge® watch was submerged 35,787 feet (10,908 m) and continued to work.

INVENTION

Inventor: Peter Henlein

Invention: Pomander watch

Date: 1510

The story: German locksmith and clockmaker Peter Henlein replaced a pendulum with a spring mechanism to create the first small spring-powered watches. These brass devices were designed to be worn as a necklace.

Smart Clothes

For thousands of years, clothes have served the important purpose of protecting our bodies from the elements. They regulate our body temperature by helping us warm up or stay cool. Today, however, clothes are getting a lot smarter. They can now communicate directly with computers and phones to identify what is happening within our bodies.

Electronic sensors can be embedded into ordinary fabrics made from cotton, wool, nylon, or polyester. They can measure things such as pulse, heart rate, body temperature, and heart rhythm, and then they send this data to a computer, smartphone, or smartwatch. Wearers can use the data to monitor their health and make adjustments needed to improve their fitness.

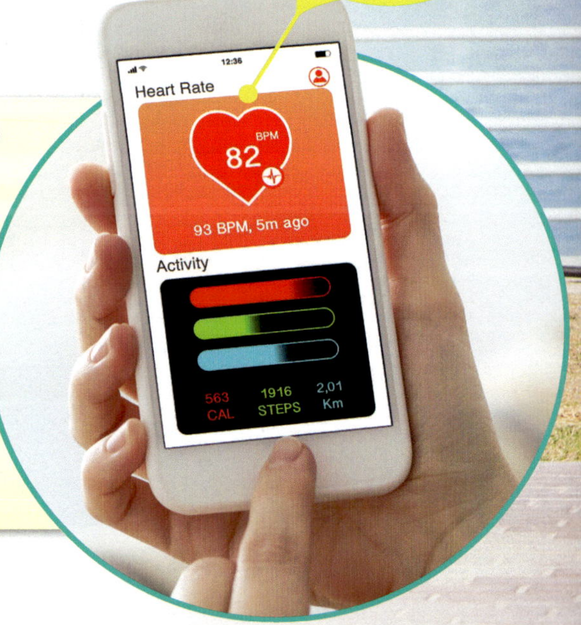

Apps can collect and summarize health data from smart clothing.

INVENTOR

Inventor: H. Lee Wainwright

Invention: The fiber-optic sweatshirt

Date: 1985

The story: Inspired by seeing a fiber-optic lamp on sale at a store, H. Lee Wainwright developed T-shirts and sweatshirts that incorporated fiber optics to create moving images of swaying palm trees, spinning car wheels, and fire-breathing dragons.

Some clothes can alert the wearer if the person is performing exercises incorrectly. Others can turn body heat into infrared light that speeds muscle recovery after hard workouts. Smart socks track speed, distance, steps, and footfall pattern. Smart swimsuits alert wearers to high UV light, reminding them to apply sunscreen. There are even some smart baby hats that record a baby's temperature and sleep patterns for new parents.

DID YOU KNOW? There are smart jackets that allow cyclists to answer calls, play music, and interact with a virtual assistant without having to use their hands.

Medical Tech

Medical technology is constantly advancing to monitor and diagnose people's health. Doctors use stethoscopes to listen to a patient's heart and thermometers to check their temperature. Blood pressure cuffs check blood pressure with two separate measurements—the systolic pressure, when the heart contracts, and the diastolic pressure, when the heart relaxes.

EKG machines send information to computers for easy analysis and retrieval.

Glucometer

A glucometer tests the amount of glucose, a type of sugar, in the blood. A sensor inside a patch takes blood readings through the skin. The sensor collects readings every 10 to 15 minutes and sends the data wirelessly to a remote monitor. If levels are not within the normal range, it triggers an alarm.

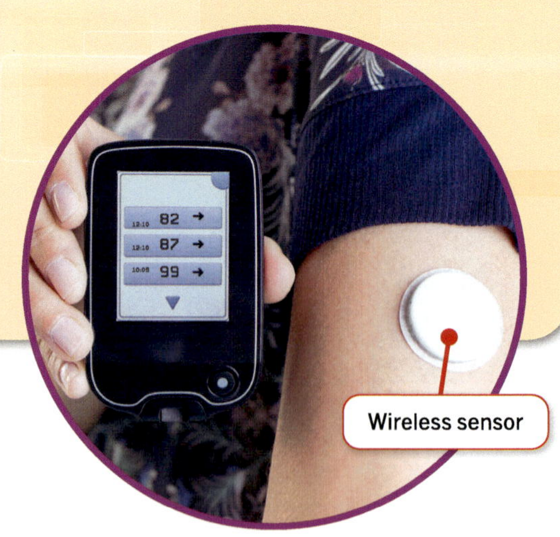

Wireless sensor

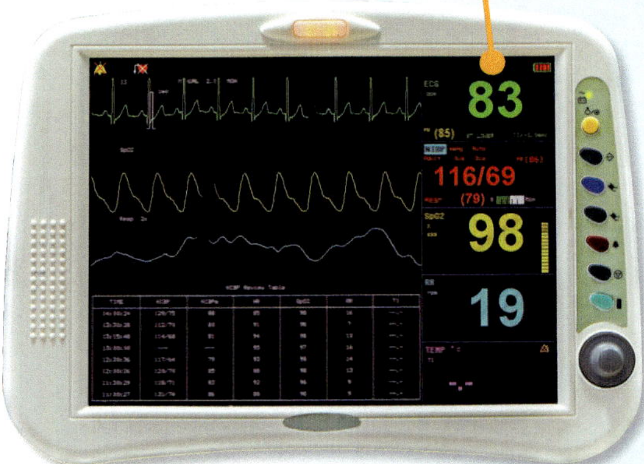

Electrocardiogram

An electrocardiogram (EKG) measures the electrical activity of the heart to help diagnose if it's healthy. Sensors attached to the skin detect electrical signals produced by the heart each time it beats. An EKG can display the heart's rhythm and activity as a line on a screen.

Blood Pressure Cuffs

1. A pump inflates the cuff around the arm to temporarily stop blood flow to the heart.
2. As the cuff is deflated, the blood flows again.
3. When the cuff pressure equals the systolic pressure, blood starts to flow past the cuff, creating vibrations recorded by the device.
4. When the cuff pressure falls below the diastolic pressure, the vibrations stop.
5. The vibrations are converted into electrical signals by a device called a transducer. They are then recorded as numbers on a display.

Systolic pressure

Diastolic pressure

INVENTOR

Inventor: René Laennec

Invention: Stethoscope

Date: 1816

The story: French physician René Laennec amplified a patient's heartbeat with a handmade wooden device. It had a flat surface at one end and a trumpet at the other. He called it the monaural stethoscope.

DID YOU KNOW? In 2013, a stethoscope was invented that enables doctors on Earth to hear the heartbeats of astronauts in space.

Pacemakers

A pacemaker is a device surgically implanted under the skin in the chest or abdomen of patients who need help maintaining their heart's regular rhythm. Electrodes, or sensors that pick up electrical signals, detect the heart's rhythm and send data through wires to a microchip in the device. If the rhythm is abnormal, the microchip directs a battery-powered generator to send electrical pulses through the wires to the heart. This fixes irregularities.

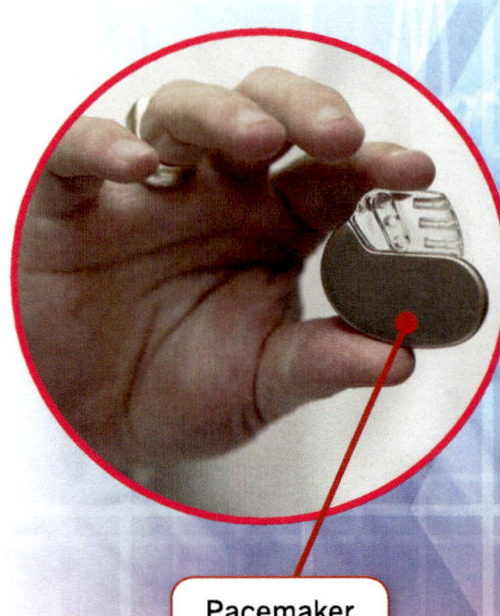

Pacemaker

Microchip

The pacemaker's microchip can learn the pattern of a patient's heart activity and adjust to support it. It can also monitor a person's blood temperature and breathing rate and automatically adjust if the patient changes their activity level.

Leadless Pacemaker

This type of pacemaker is a small device placed directly into a patient's heart through a vein in the leg. There are no wires, and its battery will last approximately 12 years. It works in the same way as a traditional pacemaker by sensing changes in the patient's body related to activity levels and adjusting the heart rate accordingly.

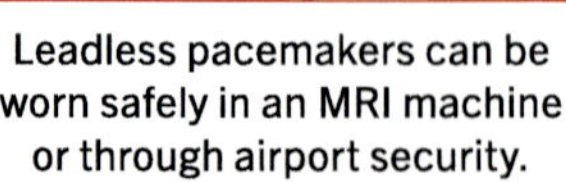

Leadless pacemakers can be worn safely in an MRI machine or through airport security.

INVENTOR

Inventor: Wilson Greatbatch

Invention: Pacemaker

Date: 1958

The story: American engineer Wilson Greatbatch invented the first successful pacemaker while trying to record the sound of a heartbeat. He used the wrong transistor, which produced a pulse with the same rhythm as the heart.

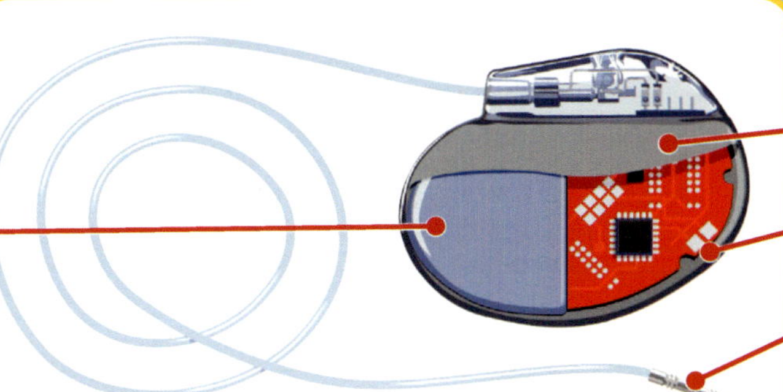

Pacemaker

The electrodes stimulate the upper and lower chambers of the heart to make them contract in a regular rhythm.

The pacemaker is sealed in a waterproof case, so no body fluids can enter.

DID YOU KNOW? Scientists are working on a pacemaker without batteries. It is powered by energy from the heart.

Prosthetic Limbs

A prosthetic limb is an artificial device used to replace a missing arm or leg. The pylon, or skeleton, of a prosthetic is made from a strong, light material such as carbon fiber or titanium. It is usually covered by foam and is often shaped to match the real limb. A prosthetic arm can be controlled by movements of the shoulder to which it is attached using a cable and harness. Some prosthetics are powered by motors that the wearer controls using toggles, switches, or buttons.

Myoelectric Prosthetics

Myoelectric prosthetics are controlled by electric signals generated in the muscles. When the muscles contract, electrodes placed on the surface of the skin measure the muscle movement and move the limb.

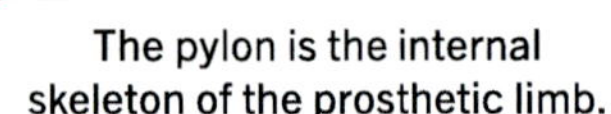

The pylon is the internal skeleton of the prosthetic limb.

DESIGNER

Designer: Sophie de Oliveira Barata

Product: Prosthetic limbs

Date: 2011

The story: Sculptor and special-effects designer Sophie de Oliveira Barata has been described as the undisputed queen of personalized prosthetics. She designs and makes fun alternative limbs, as well as realistic limbs for which she matches shape, skin tone, hair, freckles, and nails exactly.

Neural Interfacing

Some prosthetic limbs are directly controlled by the brain using neural interfacing. Tiny electrodes are placed in the brain to measure its activity. The patient thinks about the kind of movement they want to make. This generates neural signals in the brain, which are then decoded by a computer. The computer, in turn, directs the prosthetic device to perform the required movement.

DID YOU KNOW? A prosthetic tail was made for a dolphin named Winter! This new limb helped her swim again.

Artificial Hearts

The human heart carries oxygen, blood, and nutrients to all parts of a person's body. To do so, it must beat 100,000 times a day. For people with heart disease, however, sometimes the heart can no longer perform this job reliably. With the development of the artificial heart, patients are able to receive a replacement human heart.

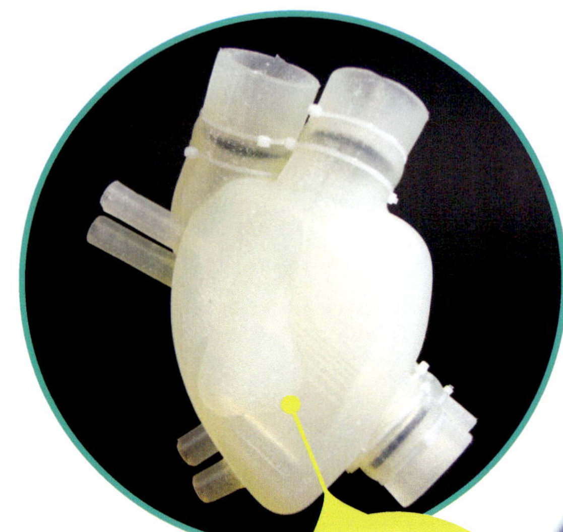

Some companies are developing soft artificial hearts that create less stress on the body.

The artificial heart is a pump that is placed within the chest and replaces diseased parts of a human heart. The pump is controlled by a machine outside the body called a driver. Patients who are able to leave the hospital receive portable drivers that can be carried in backpacks or shoulder bags.

INVENTOR

Inventor: Paul Winchell

Invention: The artificial heart

Date: 1956

The story: Better known as a popular ventriloquist and comedian, Paul Winchell patented an artificial heart that would keep a patient alive during open-heart surgery. He received help and advice from Dr. Henry Heimlich, the inventor of the anti-choking Heimlich maneuver.

Artificial hearts are built from metal and different types of plastic.

Currently, artificial hearts can be used for only a relatively short period of time, from several months to a few years. Their mechanical flow can stress and damage blood cells, causing blood clotting and strokes. In addition, the human body often rejects the devices as a foreign object. So, an artificial heart is considered a temporary measure before a patient can receive a heart transplant.

DID YOU KNOW? Researchers are developing permanent artificial hearts wrapped in biosynthetic materials to help prevent blood clots and rejection by the body.

3D Printing

A three-dimensional (3D) printer produces solid objects from a design created on a computer. First, the computer divides the 3D design into thousands of 2D layers. Then, it builds the object from the bottom up, one layer at a time. Instead of ink, the printer extrudes a material such as molten plastic or powder through a tiny nozzle that moves as directed by the computer.

3D printers can produce a huge range of products, including kitchenware, toys, and even artificial body parts.

Processes

There are different types of 3D printing. Stereolithography uses liquid resin and a laser to build objects. Ultraviolet light from the laser solidifies the resin and fuses it to the layer below. Binder 3D printing uses two separate materials—a fine powder and a liquid glue—to form each layer. The first pass lays down the powder, and the second uses nozzles to apply the glue, or binder.

In the future, we may be able to order burgers or other food from a 3D printer.

INVENTION

Inventor: Chuck Hull

Invention: Stereolithography

Date: 1983

The story: American inventor Chuck Hull is the inventor of the 3D printing process known as stereolithography. This was the world's first commercially successful, rapid 3D printing technology.

Mass Medicine

Many hospitals now have 3D printers. They are used to create medical devices, such as clamps and forceps, or to form models to assist in surgical training. 3D printers are also producing prosthetic limbs and customized bone, joint, and dental implants.

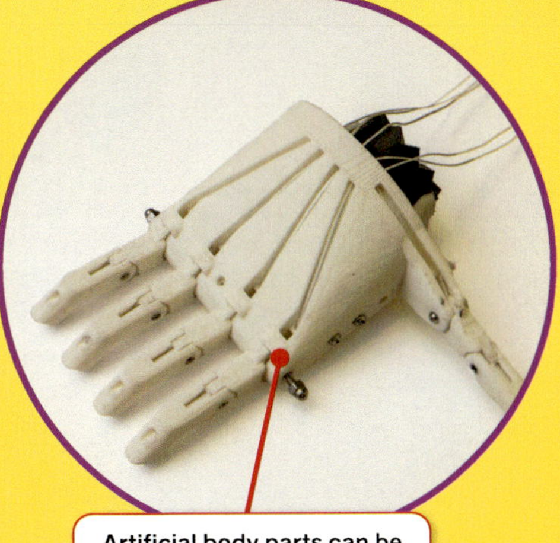

Artificial body parts can be produced by 3D printers and assembled for use.

The molten plastic or powder is guided through the tubes to the extruder.

In the extruder, the material is melted by a heating element and then pushed out, or extruded, through a nozzle.

The printing table is usually made of glass.

Motors move the printing table up and down, left and right, and backward and forward.

DID YOU KNOW? When 3D models of parts of the human body are used as guides, lengthy surgeries can be reduced by hours.

X-Ray Machines

An X-ray machine is similar to a camera, but it photographs the inside of a body. Inside an X-ray machine is a tube that contains a filament. An electric current passes through the filament to heat it, knocking electrons off the filament surface. These electrons fly through the tube, creating high-energy X-ray photons. The X-rays are then directed into a narrow beam that is passed through a patient onto a photographic plate to create an image of the patient's bones.

CAT Scanner

X-rays show just one view of the body. A computed axial tomography (CAT) scanner is a machine that creates an image of a thin portion of the body. The scanner rotates around a patient taking a series of X-rays, which are then compiled by a computer to produce an image showing the depth and position of internal structures.

CAT scan

A computer combines all the information to form detailed images.

Bones absorb X-rays so they appear white in the images.

This X-ray clearly shows where a bone is broken.

The dark areas are the soft tissues, which don't show up because X-rays pass through them.

A patient lies on the table, which slides into the ring-shaped scanner. The table moves into the scanner in stages so it can scan one small section at a time.

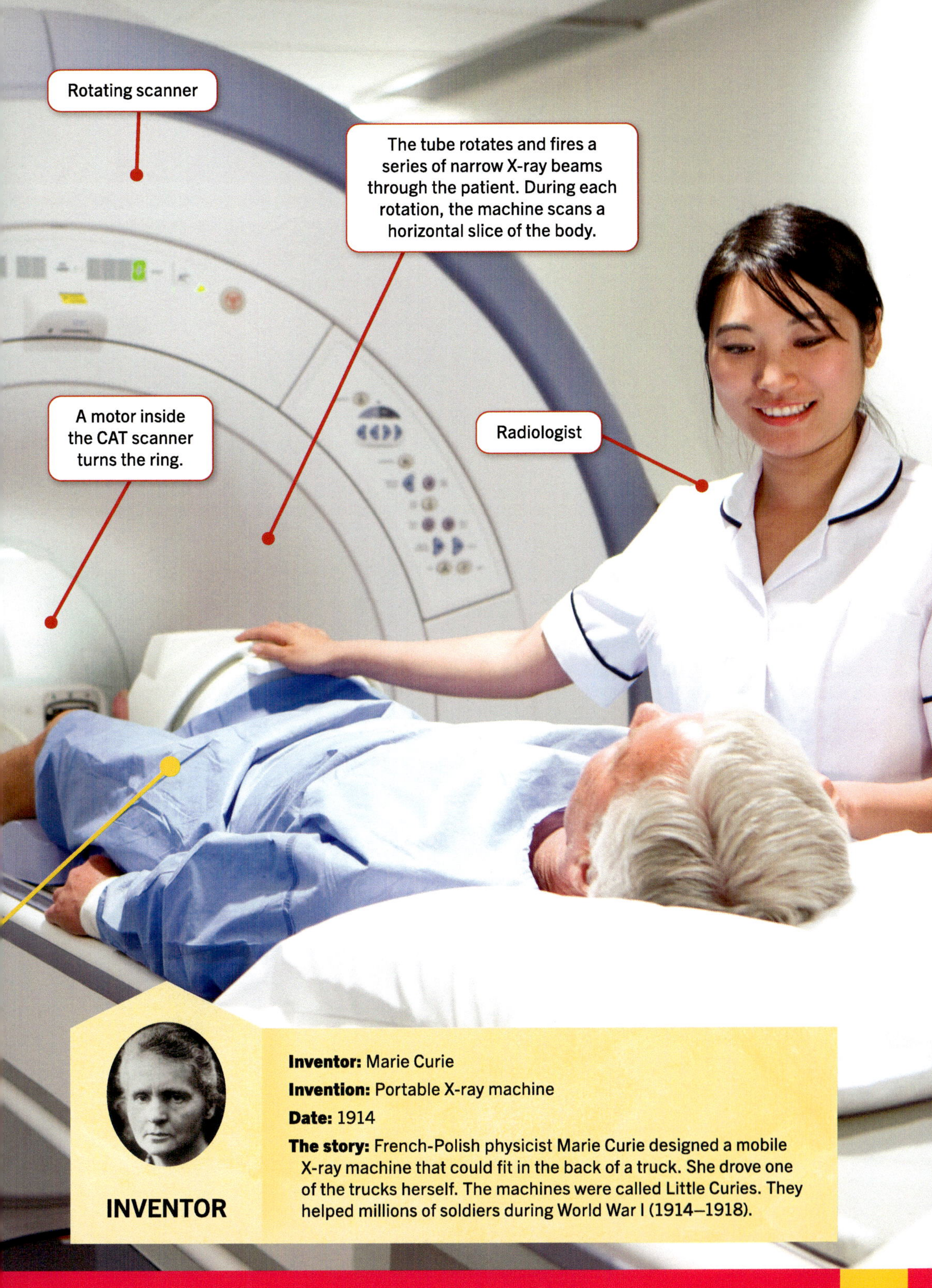

INVENTOR

Inventor: Marie Curie

Invention: Portable X-ray machine

Date: 1914

The story: French-Polish physicist Marie Curie designed a mobile X-ray machine that could fit in the back of a truck. She drove one of the trucks herself. The machines were called Little Curies. They helped millions of soldiers during World War I (1914–1918).

DID YOU KNOW? X-rays were discovered by accident in 1895 when Wilhelm Roentgen was experimenting with vacuum tubes.

MRIs

A magnetic resonance imaging (MRI) scanner uses powerful tube-shaped magnets to create a magnetic field. Protons inside the hydrogen atoms of a human body are sensitive to magnetic fields. When a patient lies under the scanner's magnets, the protons in their body line up in the same direction.

A magnetic field runs along the length of the scanner.

Radio Waves

The MRI sends out short bursts of radio waves to knock protons out of alignment. When the radio waves are turned off, the protons in different types of tissue realign at different speeds to produce distinct signals. This data is collated by a computer to produce a detailed image of the inside of a person's body. The process takes only a few seconds.

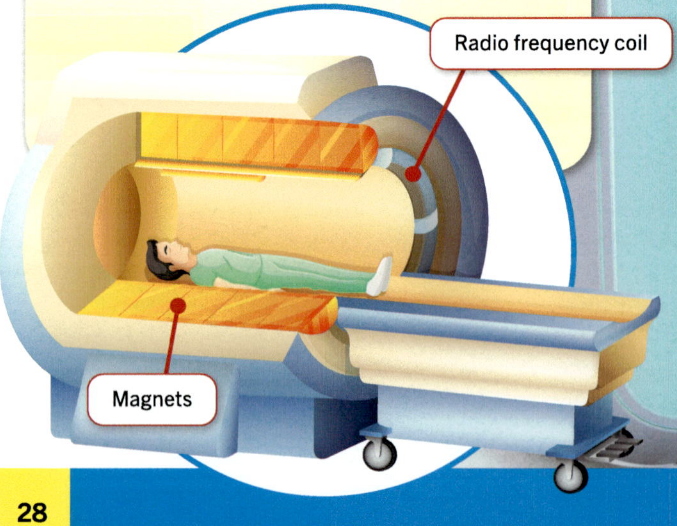

Receivers in the scanner detect the radio signals produced by the body's protons returning to their normal alignment.

INVENTOR

Inventor: Raymond Damadian

Invention: MRI scanner

Date: 1977

The story: American physician Raymond Damadian created an MRI scanner called Indomitable to diagnose cancer. He was the first person to carry out a full-body scan. The scan took five hours to complete.

The patient's whole body lies inside an MRI machine.

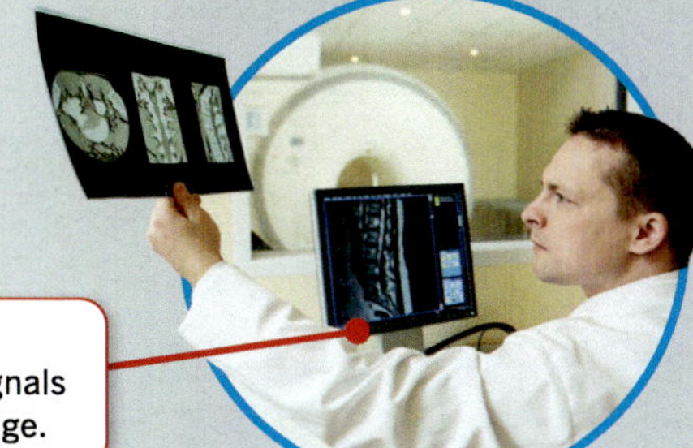

A computer processes the signals to create an image.

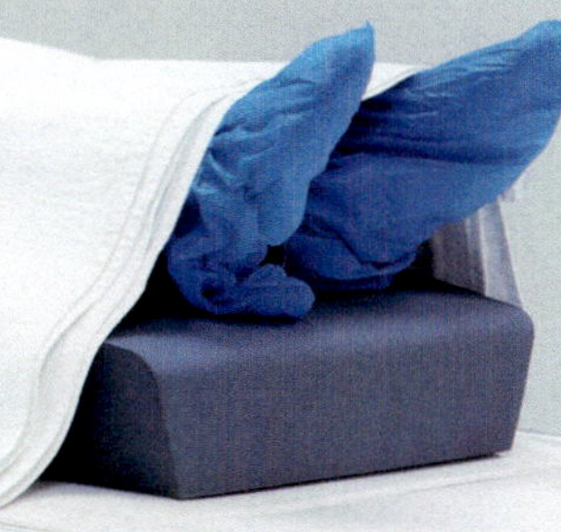

Patient

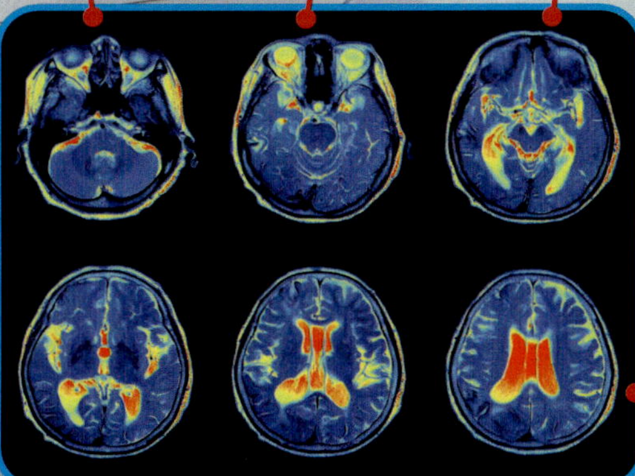

Top of the brain

Middle of the brain

Bottom of the brain

An MRI scan produces images of the body at different depths and angles.

MRI Scans

Unlike X-rays, MRI scans can show images of soft body tissues, such as those of muscles, the brain, lungs, and the liver. The scans can also detect fractures in the skeleton that are too small for X-rays to pick up.

DID YOU KNOW? The most powerful MRI scanners can create a magnetic field 140,000 times stronger than Earth's magnetic field.

Nanotechnology

Nanotechnology is the process of altering atoms and molecules. It is used to create new and improved substances or processes and to build microscopic devices. Nanoparticles are measured in nanometers, or one billionth of a meter. This is a million times smaller than an ant. Using a scanning tunneling microscope and an atomic force microscope, scientists are able to see individual atoms and alter them as needed.

Sunscreens

Nanoparticles are used in some sunscreens to make them more effective at reflecting ultraviolet light while letting visible light through. Since nanoparticles are transparent and smaller than the particles in traditional sunscreens, there is no white residue and they start working immediately to protect the skin.

Nanotechnology can reconstruct brain cells to restore cognitive function.

In the future, nanotechnology could be used to make new connections between cells.

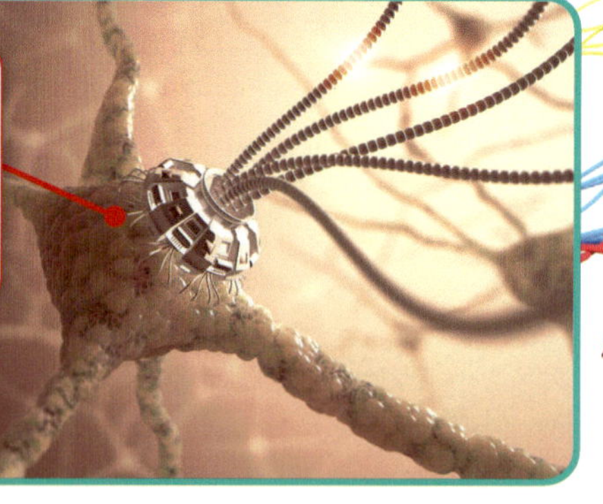

PIONEER

Pioneer: Dr. Richard Feynman

Idea: Nanotechnology

Date: 1959

The story: American physicist Dr. Richard Feynman gave a lecture entitled "There's Plenty of Room at the Bottom," which theorized about the possibility of manipulating individual atoms and molecules. This lecture was given decades before the technology was actually available.

DID YOU KNOW? Scientists have designed a fluorescent nanoparticle that glows inside the body. It is used to help identify cancer cells and organ damage.

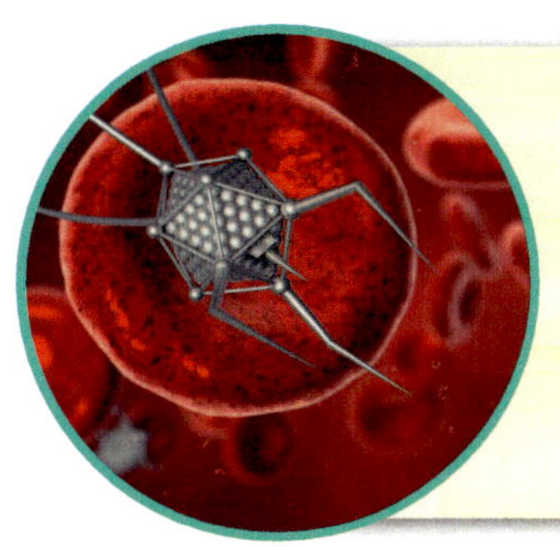

Nanoswimmers

Researchers are developing an elastic polypyrrole nanowire that can move through body fluids. These nanoswimmers can be magnetically controlled to move through the bloodstream to target cancer cells or deliver medication.

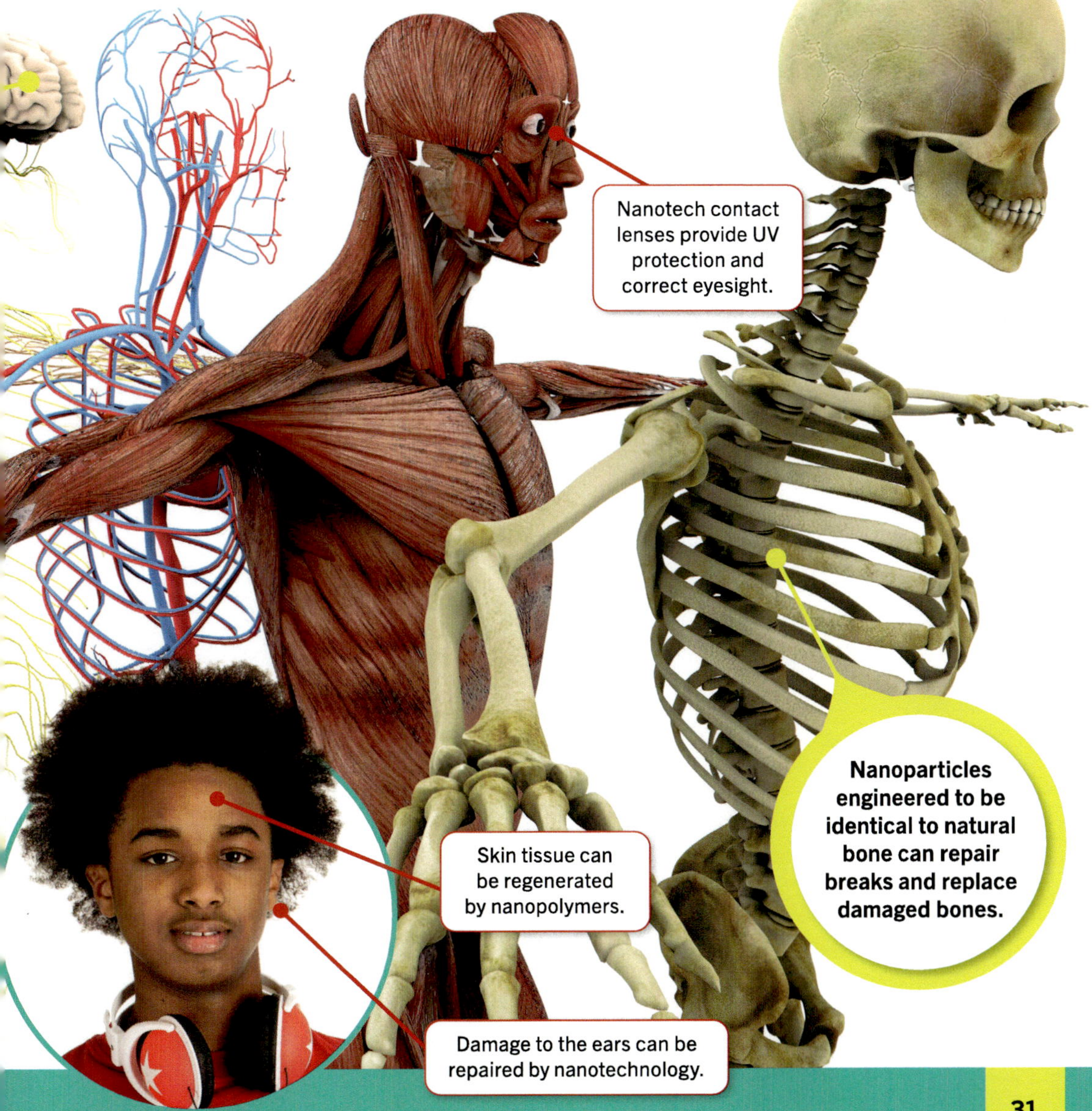

Nanotech contact lenses provide UV protection and correct eyesight.

Nanoparticles engineered to be identical to natural bone can repair breaks and replace damaged bones.

Skin tissue can be regenerated by nanopolymers.

Damage to the ears can be repaired by nanotechnology.

Microchips

Microchips are the brains of electronic devices. They are integrated circuits etched onto silicon wafers. Silicon is used because it can either conduct or contain electricity. The circuits, which are transistors and wiring built onto the chip, convert electrical signals into data in the form of on/off pulses. Microchips are now being implanted into some people to deliver medicine, provide identification and security access, and even pay for purchases.

Microchips can be very small.

Two rows of pins connect the microchip to the circuit board and conduct electronic signals.

The electronic parts are protected by a plastic case.

A single microchip can contain billions of transistors.

Microchip Medicine

Some people are having microchips implanted within their bodies to deliver targeted and time-released medications and to provide doctors with easy access to digital medical records.

DID YOU KNOW? Scientists are working on producing microchips the size of molecules.

INVENTOR

Inventor: Jeri Ellsworth

Invention: Retro gaming joystick

Date: 2004

The story: Video game developer Jeri Ellsworth taught herself chip design. She created a joystick that contained a microchip with 30 retro video games on it. It was a hit with gamers.

Silicon is manufactured as long crystals, which are then sliced into thin disks known as wafers.

The wafers are heated and coated in silicon dioxide and then exposed to ultraviolet light to add a hard, protective layer.

Electronic circuits are etched on the wafer by adding chemicals to change the composition of certain parts of the surface.

RFID Tags

Radio frequency identification (RFID) tags are devices that store and update data about a person, animal, or object. They can transmit this information to an RFID reader using radio waves. RFID tags can be attached to products being bought and sold. They can be embedded within credit cards, travel passes, and smartphones, and they are also often implanted in pets in case the animals are lost.

What do they contain?

RFID tags that are implanted in pets are about the size of a grain of rice. They are enclosed in a non-toxic capsule. Inside the capsule is a microchip that holds an ID number and other data, a capacitor, and a copper coil antenna to send and receive radio signals.

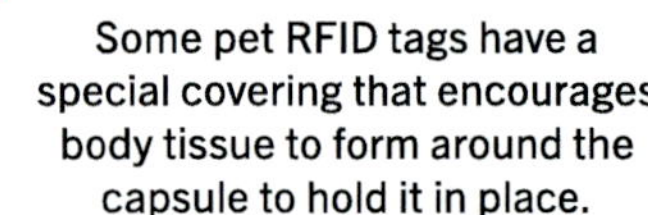
Some pet RFID tags have a special covering that encourages body tissue to form around the capsule to hold it in place.

INVENTION

Inventor: Charles Walton

Invention: RFID tag

Date: 1973

The story: American designer Charles Walton designed a portable radio frequency transmitter that stored an identification number to unlock a door without a key. It sent a signal to the reader located by the door. This technology is the basis of the RFID tag.

How do they work?

A pet RFID tag doesn't have a battery. The tag remains dormant until activated by an RFID reader. When the reader emits radio waves that energize the capacitor, it powers the microchip. The microchip then transmits the pet's ID number to the reader via the antenna, and this information is displayed on the reader's screen.

DID YOU KNOW? RFID technology is being used to monitor and help protect many endangered wild animals.

CRISPR Technology

Fruits and vegetables can be genetically altered to be more resistant to drought and insects.

Many bacteria possess an immune system that enables them to detect and destroy the DNA of a virus that is attacking them. A new technology, known as CRISPR, exploits this ability of bacteria in order to make changes to DNA and works toward a cure for genetic diseases. CRISPR enables cells to record those viruses they have been exposed to and pass protection on through DNA over many generations.

Cas9

Part of the CRISPR system is a protein called Cas9, which is able to seek out, cut, and degrade virus DNA. Scientists have harnessed Cas9's ability as a means of deleting or inserting pieces of DNA into the DNA helix with absolute precision.

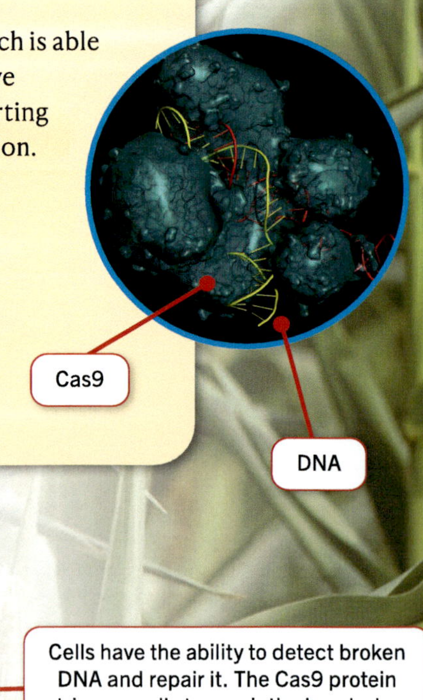

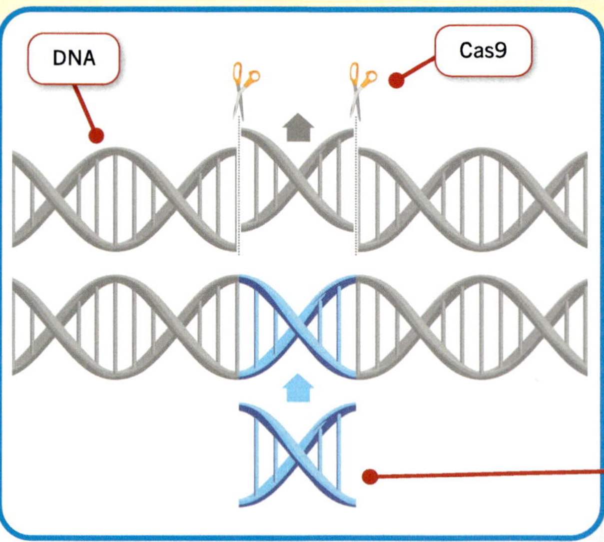

Cells have the ability to detect broken DNA and repair it. The Cas9 protein triggers cells to repair the breaks by integrating new genetic information.

DID YOU KNOW? By targeting cancerous cells in mice using CRISPR technology, scientists have stopped and reduced the cancer's growth.

INVENTOR

Inventor: Emmanuelle Charpentier (*pictured*) and Jennifer Doudna

Invention: CRISPR

Date: 2012

The story: French microbiologist and geneticist Emmanuelle Charpentier and American biochemist Jennifer Doudna discovered CRISPR-Cas9 while doing a basic research project aimed at finding out how bacteria fight viral infections.

Robots

Robots are programmable machines that interact with the physical world. Their bodies are made up of movable segments of metal or plastic connected by joints. Some robots move using an actuator, a part of a machine that generates the force needed for movement. It responds to a control signal that may be an electric current, a pneumatic or hydraulic pressure, or even human power.

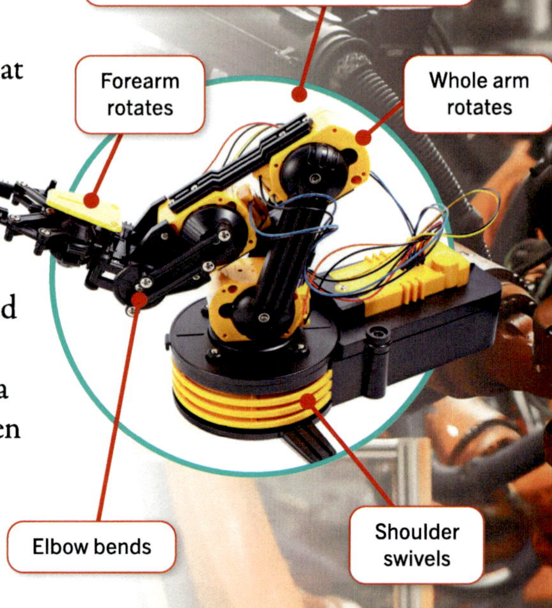

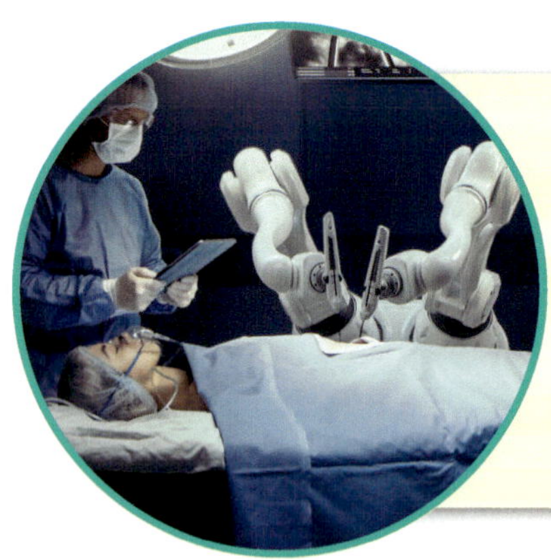

Dr. Robot

Robots are increasingly being used to support human health. They assist doctors performing surgery, deliver targeted radiation to treat cancer, disinfect hospital rooms, and deliver hospital supplies, linens, and meals. Some robots even provide companionship and emotional support to patients.

INVENTION

Inventor: George Devol

Invention: Robotic arm

Date: 1961

The story: American inventor George Devol designed a mechanical arm that could be programmed to repeat precise tasks such as grasping and lifting. His invention revolutionized production lines around the world.

Swarm Robots

Today, scientists are creating and testing tiny swarm robots. These identical robots communicate using infrared light to work together in order to carry out tasks, similar to bee and ant colonies. Some can also connect to one another to make a single, larger machine.

DID YOU KNOW? A robotic exoskeleton can help people who have been paralyzed walk. Nurses can also wear them to lift and carry heavy items.

Artificial Intelligence

Sophia the robot is programmed to learn and improve.

Artificial intelligence (AI) is the use of data and computer algorithms to learn patterns and perform tasks that usually require human intelligence, such as problem-solving or logical reasoning. First, a computer gathers lots of data. This can be done through sensors or human input. Then, the AI program compares this to stored data, detects and identifies patterns, and produces a result or decides on a course of action. AI allows computers to perform tasks much more quickly than humans.

Computer chess engines can analyze hundreds of millions of moves per second, enabling them to beat human grand masters.

Machine Learning

Sometimes, computers are used to identify patterns and anomalies in a mass of data. This can be used to identify spam emails, financial fraud, objects in an image, or certain words in speech. The computers need to make decisions based on probability. This form of AI is called machine learning, because it can learn and improve from experience without being programmed to do so. One problem, however, is that the programs often repeat the biases of their human programmers.

Humanoid Robots

Some robots are built to look and act like humans. Pepper was the first humanoid robot capable of recognizing human emotions and adapting its responses accordingly. It can work in hospitals to monitor, visit with, and entertain patients.

Sophia is able to display more than 60 facial expressions.

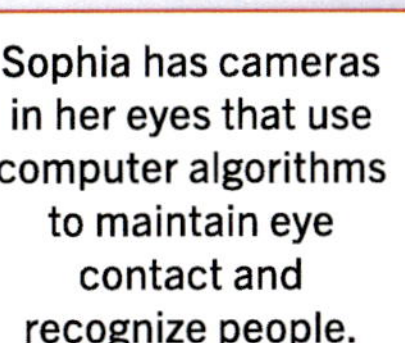

Sophia has cameras in her eyes that use computer algorithms to maintain eye contact and recognize people.

Pepper expresses itself through arm movements and by changing the color of its eyes, words on its tablet, and the tone of its voice.

Sophia can process speech and have conversations using natural language.

INVENTOR

Inventor: Herbert A. Simon (*pictured*) and Allen Newell

Invention: General Problem Solver

Date: 1958

The story: Herbert A. Simon and Allen Newell created the General Problem Solver, a computer program that solved problems through trial and error by analyzing end results. It was a major step toward AI.

DID YOU KNOW? AI and computer sensors are being used together to stop infections in hospitals by alerting doctors and nurses if they haven't washed their hands adequately.

What Tech Can Do for the Future

Technology is always changing and innovating. Even 200 years ago, there were no antibiotics to treat infections, no medications to lower blood pressure or cholesterol, no X-rays or MRIs to diagnose cancer, and no chemotherapy or radiation therapy to treat it. Doctors did not know they should wash their hands before surgery—or even that germs existed!

Before the end of the 21st century, we can expect many more changes. Doctors may be using augmented reality to help them perform surgeries, robotic pills could deliver targeted medications inside the body, and genetic testing might even allow us to identify diseases long before they start.

In the future, robots may be fully integrated into our health care systems, providing both physical and emotional support.

Some experts believe emerging medical technologies will someday allow humans to live healthy lives that last 150 years or more. What kinds of new medical devices can you dream up to improve or extend life? With a lot of studying, hard work, and testing, maybe you will make that dream a reality!

Review and Reflect

Now that you've read about the technology used for health and the human body, let's review what you've learned. Use the following questions to reflect on your newfound knowledge and integrate it with what you already knew.

Check for Understanding

1. What are convex lenses? What are concave lenses? What do people use them for? *(See pp. 6–7)*

2. Explain how both analog and digital hearing aids work. *(See pp. 10–11)*

3. What does an electric circuit do inside a watch? *(See pp. 12–13)*

4. What can sensors inside clothing do? *(See pp. 14–15)*

5. Which two measurements does a blood pressure cuff take? *(See pp. 16–17)*

6. What is a pacemaker? What does it do? *(See pp. 18–19)*

7. Name at least two materials used to make prosthetic limbs. *(See pp. 20–21)*

8. List at least three things that a 3D printer can manufacture. *(See pp. 24–25)*

9. In what ways are X-rays and CAT scans similar? What is different about them? *(See p. 26–27)*

10. What do MRI scans collect images of? *(See pp. 28–29)*

11. What can nanotechnology do now? What might it be able to do in the future? *(See pp. 30–31)*

12. Describe a microchip. What can it be used for? *(See pp. 32–33)*

13. What does RFID stand for? What does this type of device do? *(See pp. 34–35)*

14. How is CRISPR technology related to disease? How is it related to food? *(See pp. 36–37)*

15. List at least two tasks a robot can do. *(See pp. 38–39)*

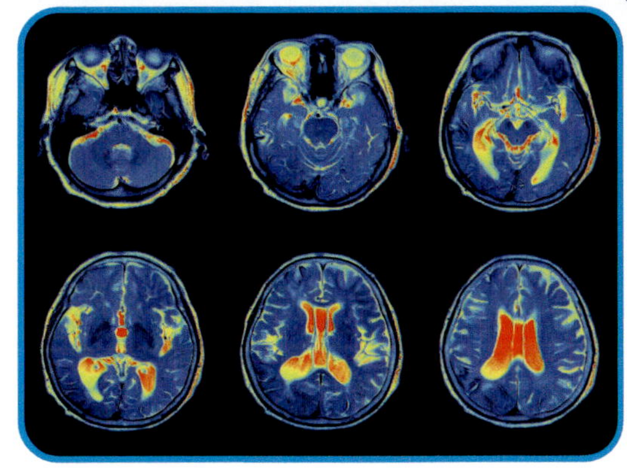

Making Connections

1. Compare and contrast X-ray machines and MRI scanners.
2. How does the size of a type of technology inform what it can do? What can tiny tech devices do? What about bigger technology?
3. Some of the tools and devices mentioned in this book are inserted or injected into a human or animal body. Choose at least two of these to compare and contrast.
4. Choose two inventors mentioned in the book. In your own words, describe what they made. How did their work affect society? What do their inventions have in common?
5. Pick an older invention mentioned in this book. How has it evolved over time?

In Your Own Words

1. Choose one type of smart tech described in the book. What do you see as the benefits of using it? What are some possible drawbacks to using it?
2. What health-related job would you like technology to do that it can't yet? What are the steps that might be needed to develop this technology?
3. Which technology described in this book surprised you the most? Why?
4. Why do you think scientists and engineers continue to make new technology for human bodies?
5. Which of the tools or inventions listed in the book are most relevant to your life? Why? Are there parts of your life where you think you need more or less tech?

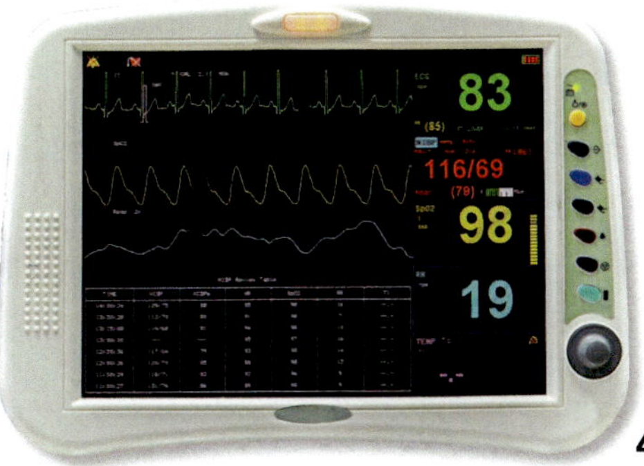

Glossary

amplifier a device for increasing the amplitude of electrical signals, especially in sound reproduction

capacitor a device used to store an electrical charge

concave having a surface that curves inward, like the interior of a sphere

convex having a surface that curves outward, like the exterior of a sphere

DNA deoxyribonucleic acid; material present in nearly all living organisms that carries genetic information

electron a particle within an atom that carries a negative charge

extrude to force out through a nozzle

filament a piece of thin, coiled wire

frequency the number of times a wave completes a cycle in a second

friction the resistance that one surface or object encounters when moving over another

induction the production of an electric current by being close to, but not touching, an electrified or magnetized body

infrared having a wavelength greater than that of the red end of the visible light spectrum but less than that of microwaves

laser a device that generates an intense beam of light through the emission of photons from excited atoms or molecules

magnetic field a region around a magnet within which the force of magnetism acts

photon a particle representing a discrete quantity of light

prosthetic artificial, as in a body part

proton a particle within an atom that carries a positive charge

radiation the emission of energy in the form of electromagnetic waves

tomography a technique for displaying a cross-section through a human body or some other solid object using X-rays or ultrasound

transistor a tiny device that can amplify or switch an electronic signal

ultraviolet having a wavelength shorter than that of the violet end of visible light, but longer than that of X-rays

vacuum a space from which the air has been removed

Read More

Greek, Joe. *Working with Tech in Health Care (Technology in the Workplace).* New York: Rosen Publishing, 2020.

Gutiérrez, Jolene. *Bionic Beasts: Saving Animal Lives with Artificial Flippers, Legs, and Beaks.* Minneapolis: Millbrook Press, 2021.

Hulick, Kathryn. *What Is Artificial Intelligence? (Artificial Intelligence).* Lake Elmo, MN: Focus Readers, 2020.

Nardo, Don. *The Medical Revolution: How Technology Is Changing Health Care.* San Diego: ReferencePoint Press, 2021.

Learn More Online

1. Go to **www.factsurfer.com** or scan the QR code below.
2. Enter "**Body Health Tech**" into the search box.
3. Click on the cover of this book to see a list of websites.

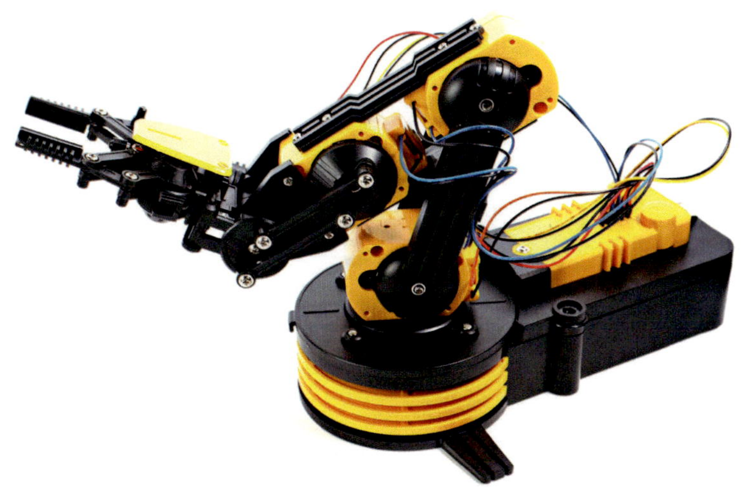

Index